Special Strength

Lessons from Livia

Brandon LaRue

D1316699

Copyright © 2020 Brandon LaRue

All rights reserved.

ISBN: 9798642109182

DEDICATION

This book is dedicated to my daughter, Livia. Outside of loving the snot out of her, I wanted to do something truly special for her. Whether one person reads it or one million people read it, it matters not. Writing this has been one of my life's greatest joys and like many people in this world that don't have the ability to speak, their story needs to be heard. Life is fleeting, and Livia teaches me so much about how to live life present and for the right reasons. We never know how much time we have with the cherished people in our lives, and I often wonder how much more time I get with Livia. It hurts to think about it, but then I'm reminded we get eternity because of Jesus.

CONTENTS

	Dedication	Pg 3
	Forewards	Pg 6 - 14
	Preface	Pg 15 – 17
	Acknowledgements	Pg 18 - 19
	Introduction	Pg 22-25
1	Chapter: Patience	Pg 25 - 29
2	Chapter Surrender	Pg 30 – 34
3	Chapter Work	Pg 35 – 38
4	Chapter Medication	Pg 39 – 42
5	Chapter Challenge	Pg 43 – 45
6	Chapter Crippling	Pg 46 – 49
7	Chapter Control	Pg 50 – 52
8	Chapter Serial Casting	Pg 53 – 56
9	Chapter Fascination	Pg 57 – 59
10	Chapter Listen	Pg 60 – 62
11	Chapter: Atrophy	Pg 63 – 65

12	Chapter: Stare	Pg 66 – 70
13	Chapter: Supercompensation	Pg 71 – 75
14	Chapter: Communication	Pg 76 – 80
15	Chapter: Empathy	Pg 81 – 83
16	Chapter: Nourishment	Pg 84 – 89
17	Chapter: Enemy	Pg 90 - 93
18	Chapter: Focus	Pg 94 - 97
19	Chapter: Loneliness	Pg 98 - 102
20	Chapter: Love	Pg 103 - 106

FORWARDS

Special Strength: Lessons from Livia will help you LIVE!
Jesus gave Brandon and Jenny, Livia! Beautifully and
wonderfully made! To know Liv, as we affectionately call
her, is to know LOVE! This little girl has a quiet strength,
a special strength about her. And she draws you in, closer.

Liv's life is a life of joy and a life of struggle. It's how she
connects with you. In her struggle she finds joy through
her Mom and Dad, through Brooks and Bradie, and for
those who look past the disability and to her beauty, she
finds joy in us, too! She lets you into her world and helps
you see joy, joy that you can have too. Life struggles are
just life lessons and how we approach them define us. For
Liv, casts hurt but are needed, feeding tubes and surgeries
go hand in hand, exam room pokes and prods are
frequent, wheelchairs need to be adjusted, and bottles for
nourishment are all part of the drill in the life of Liv. Liv
challenges us to live everyday as she does, by persevering,
by being who you were meant to be each day.

Liv didn't choose her life, but she chooses each day to Liv
her life! Liv sings with her Daddo on Facebook, laughs
with her siblings as they play with her, cuddles with her
Mom, Jenny, when she feeds her, and smiles when she is
happy, which is almost all of the time. But she has her
down moments, too, like we all do. Liv's lessons will help
teach you how to overcome your barriers, your limitations,
and gain wisdom in the struggle because like Liv, your life
is and will be difficult, but it can also be a tremendous
blessing, too. Learn the lessons in this book for

7

encouragement, feel free to cry with the setbacks, but move forward with joy as she and you make progress as Liv shows us all how to have that joy!

Liv's smile is contagious, and you want more if it. Her strength seems limitless, and you want to discover it. Her love of God and from God is flawless, and I am amazed by it! How do I know? As Dawn and I are around Liv a lot, she "talks" to us, follows us, and focuses and searches for us when we talk with her, and then she responds to us. She connects with us because she is intentional! With God, when we are in church, she sings! She connects with God, in her own way, incomprehensible to us, but fully understood by the Lord above, I am convinced! Liv's faith is amazing! We pray more for her AND because of her, which draws us closer to God, a life lesson from Liv that may be the most beautiful lesson of them all!

Lastly, in this book, you will find the heart of Liv through the words of Brandon. Mijo, I am amazed by you. You show the love of a father for his daughter in all her beauty and all your compassion. I've seen your heartache as a father replaced by inspiration by a daughter who may not be able to lift a kettlebell, but through this book, will lift the spirits of all who read it. Liv's Special Strength transcends all understanding and shows us when we apply the lessons from Liv, her strength becomes ours, too. Let *Special Strength: Lessons from Livia* sink in and inspire you. Learn from her, pray for her, Liv for her, and live life better because of Liv.

Be Blessed,

Ray and Dawn Martinez

Christ Followers and Life travelers with the LaRues

When Brandon asked us to write the foreword for his book, our immediate response was, "Of course!" Brandon, Jenny, and their beautiful children are family to us. We would do anything for them. After feeling humbled and honored, other feelings started creeping in, you know the ones; anxiety, fear, and comparison. You see though, Livia and Brandon speak to these exact feelings in this book. Its pages are filled with profound, yet simple, lessons applicable to everyday life by two of the most incredible, well-built humans we know.

Sam and Brandon played baseball together in college. However, it wasn't until years later, when they reconnected that we would realize the life-changing impact Brandon (and Jenny) would have on our family. They are different. They are different in the way they carry themselves. They are different in the way they speak life into others. They are different in their obedience to the Lord, and if you spend even the slightest amount of time with them, you will want to be different, too.

Livia Jean came into this world destined to be different. The impact she will make on this world will have a ripple effect far-reaching. Throughout this book, infinite wisdom is shared as Livia teaches Brandon different life lessons. Some lessons, he may have already learned, but needed reminding; other lessons are new while they navigate Livia's epilepsy diagnosis. Each lesson is unique, challenging, and perspective-shifting at the same time. Each lesson is filled with truth and transparent moments.

Our prayer is that the pages of this book will challenge you to be different, as Brandon, Jenny, and Livia have challenged us. Our prayer is that you will not only read this book, but share it, as well. There are lost souls who desperately need these Lessons from Livia. Lastly, we pray abundant blessings and many more lessons from Livia for the LaRue family.

Sam and Eva Hoppe

First, let me start by saying that my husband (JP) and I love the LaRue family deeply so there may be a bit of bias to how much we love this book and the lessons and truth it puts forth. But, then again, the fact that we love them is probably why we have the humbling honor of writing a foreword to, what I believe, is the first of several books to be written by Brandon and inspired by sweet Livia.

Simply put, this book will make you a better person...no joke! Of course it will be up to YOU to take the Lessons from Livia and apply them to your own life. However, I firmly believe that hearing Livia's story and how Brandon and Jenny have used adversity to grow, love and impact others, will give you the motivation and confidence to seek and cultivate the best version of yourself.

If there is only one thing I hope you take away from this book (but I guarantee it will be so much more), it is a complete picture of how PERFECT Livia LaRue is! I tear up as I write this because I have thought so many times as I sat by her, talked to her, held her, heard her laugh, heard her cry, or had her look into my eyes, that she is absolutely perfect! Maybe not in the traditional sense, but in the fact that she has never sinned, never hurt anyone, never judged anyone, never battled with temptation, never battled with self-defeating behaviors (and the list goes on and on) which is astoundingly similar to the most perfect being to ever walk this earth, Jesus Christ. Now don't you want to learn from someone like that?! I know I do and already have ten times over.

Get ready to fall in love with Livia and fall in love with the LaRue family. I know I did!

JP & Angela Penzkover

Special Strength: Lessons from Livia, is a truly inspirational story! Through tears and cheers, this journey will lead you to the very heart of God. There are many life lessons learned through Livia Jean, and I have no doubt you will walk away striving to be a better person after reading this book.

I was blessed to meet the LaRue family when Livia started her first year of preschool. Little did I know the impact this little girl would have on my heart and how she would forever change who I am. During the school year, while working with Livia, she showed me in her own unique way what everyday strength, determination and pure love looks like. When you look beyond Livia's disability, you see the perfectly beautiful child God created, and can't help but to want to be better in your own life.

Livia's beautiful traits come from her devoted parents, Brandon and Jenny. Through their acts of faith, understanding, and patience, Brandon and Jenny give their imperfectly, perfect daughter never-ending love. Brandon and Jenny leave us wanting to do better and be better. It's inspiring, it's joyful and most importantly, it's contagious! Brandon shares Livia's inspiring story of struggles and strength, giving us a new hope that anything is possible with God. God gave Brandon and Jenny their daughter, Livia, to make a difference in all of us and she is doing just that! Livia Jean is changing our world, one person at a time!

-Ms. Erica (Hubers)
Livia's Preschool Educational Assistant

To say I was honored when Brandon asked me to write a foreword for his book would be an understatement. I have always admired my brother's drive and compassion for others, but reading *Special Strength: Lessons from Livia* has brought that to a whole newfound level of respect and admiration. It is a beautifully written and captivating book that is raw and honest. It is filled with lessons on faith, strength, love, patience and perseverance. Witnessing Brandon and Jenny as parents to their beautiful children is so inspiring. They provide faith-filled and steadfast love, even in the hardest of times. I could not be more proud of them, and the amazing example they are setting.

I am Auntie Mamie to Liv, her brother, Brooks, and sister, Bradie. It is truly one of my most treasured titles. I've adored Liv since the first time I held her in my arms. In the beginning, there was the simple fear for her well-being. Then came the sadness for all of the things that she would be unable to do, along with my own personal fears and self-doubt, that I would not know how to properly care for her. However; the more time I have spent with Liv, she has taught me so much! I am able to see all of her blessings and strengths, instead of my perceived weaknesses. She is tiny, but she is so mighty and the most courageous person I have ever met. Quiet by words, she can say more with one look with those big, soulful, brown eyes. Her coos, smiles, and laughter can light up any room she occupies. She brings immense joy into the hearts of anyone in her presence.

I no longer see Liv as my niece with special needs, but my niece with special strengths! In almost five years of time spent with Liv, she has truly changed my perspective on life. To embrace the challenges and struggles, and always persevere. Stop worrying about all the what ifs, and be present and find joy in each day we are given. Never take anything for granted, because God has a plan, and he always provides.

I pray that this book speaks to your heart like it did mine. Everyone has a lesson to learn from Livia Jean LaRue. This girl is going to move mountains!

Blessings and Love,

Jamie Vix (Auntie Mamie)

PREFACE

I am a pretty active and transparent guy on social media about the topics of life of which I am passionate about. When Livia was born and the complications and unique needs began, it was clear that you truly cannot prepare for such a life event. But amongst all the uncertainty around that situation, Livia began revealing to me, along with God Almighty, powerful perspectives and wisdom. So I began sharing these little pearls on Facebook, and they began going viral and I found out real quickly that *Livia's Lessons* not only connected with me, but they really connected with just about everyone. Soon after that, people kept saying, "Brandon, you should write a book." I was flattered by the compliments and encouragement. I'm not sure why I've procrastinated this long, because my answer to everyone's suggestion to writing this book was always, "I will."

While the world will want to identify Livia as a child with "special needs," the creator of the universe identifies her as a perfect and wonderful creation that will impact the world in profound ways. She is a daughter of God in Heaven and has been given as a most precious gift to my wife and I. As much as we get the honor and privilege to take care of and lead this incredible little girl that is as rare as painite, the rarest gemstone in the world, she teaches us what is real and important in life. The term "special needs" does not define her. Here is a revelation I have had about being a parent of a child with special needs and having been in the business of helping people for a long time:

Who doesn't have "special needs?" Take a moment and ponder that thought for a minute.

I have special needs that need to be tended to. You have special needs that you need tending to. So let's all adopt a fresh and new perspective about the term "special needs" and whenever you see a person that literally has what the world defines as "special needs," remember that you are their equal, a person with special needs.

If there's one single take away from this entire book, it is this:

Do not get caught up in what the world thinks of you in this life, but let your mind, heart, and soul be transformed by what God wants for you in this life. And trust me my friend (can I call you that, yet?), He wants so much good to blossom in your life. (Romans 12:2)

16

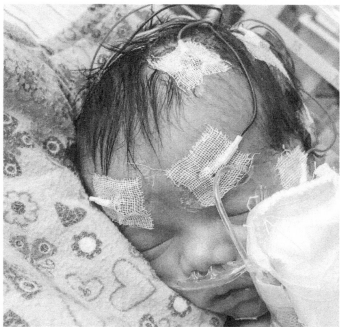

1: This is where the lessons all began. This is the image that absolutely broke me as a man and a father. But I broke in the best way, and Livia's lessons, which I believe are divinely inspired by the Lord, have been building me up ever since.

ACKNOWLEDGMENTS

Where do we even begin? We'll start with thanking
everyone who ever encouraged us to write this book.
There are too many people to remember, but Livia and I
both want you to know that we started, persevered, and
finished this together because of your encouragement. You
know who you are, and we thank you!

We also want to thank all the people who have prayed for
Livia. The power of prayer is real, and we are so grateful
for those prayers. Additionally, we are so grateful for the
love that has been expressed to Livia. Every child deserves
the amount of love and life spoken over their children
which has been done for Livia. Your love is etched inside
of this book.

Lastly, and certainly not least, we need to thank Momma.
Words cannot quite describe how beautiful Jennifer is as a
wife, mother, and friend. This book simply would never
have come to fruition if it weren't for her. The Lord
blessed Jenny and I with Livia, but the Lord first blessed
me with Jenny. She's our everything.

2: My Darlin, My Queen, My Bride, and the Love of my life, Jenny. She is a blessing to anyone she meets, and she has blessed me with her steadfast love and 3 amazing children. Behind Jesus, she is the biggest reason we have such a SPECIAL LIFE!

INTRODUCTION

You are flawed, yet you are special. You are messed up, but you are wonderful. You carry a lot of baggage, and in carrying it for so long, you have actually become stronger; you just don't know it yet.

So let's pack some of that baggage up, throw it on our back and squat it, press it, deadlift it, and we will get so stinkin' strong emotionally, mentally, and physically and finally realize that everything has been working for us all this time—not against us. Romans 8:28 states, "...and we know that in all things God works for the good of those who love him, who have been called according to his purpose."

This book will likely be unlike anything you have ever read before. Mostly because Livia and I have no idea how to compose and organize a book; I'm only kidding, I guess we have made it this far! Truthfully though, I am a strength and nutrition coach/entrepreneur by trade, and Livia is a four-year-old little girl, but Livia and I did not let that stop us from figuring it out. In this book, we will bounce around from one idea to the next, sometimes in rhythm and sometimes scatter-brained-like, but always coming to a valuable point. Before we begin, let us all just get our hearts positioned correctly from the get-go. You will have to get used to the fact that we are going to address some things that make most people squirm. In fact, we are going to tackle a lot of uncomfortable things together. If you are all about being lazy, selfish, complacent, and living an average existence, then just close up shop right now and hand this book to someone else. While you are at it, if you are a guy, kick yourself in the nuts, and if you are a woman, umm, do whatever is comparable to a guy kicking himself in the nuts.

If you are still with us, we'll assume you didn't do any self-harm, and you're ready to go on this journey with Livia and I. Assuming we are on the same page, then here is what we ask of you. We ask that you finish what you start. Chances are, you have become like most people who intend to do well, but just struggle walking the walk and finishing what you start. Good intentions are like a husband telling his wife on their anniversary, "I intended to get you flowers." Husbands, let me know how that one turns out. So let us commit together to not just "intend" to finish this together. Commit to finishing. The very act of starting something and then finishing it will actually reinforce your neurological system to then go start and finish something else! Don't believe me? Google it!

I'm not going to waste your time or mine finding research to back up all the points we're about to make in this book, because anyone can cherry pick anything from the interwebs, cite it, and make themselves look smarter than they appear. The ironic thing about all that, is that I am a science guy. I earned my Master's in Science, so I have an appreciation for it, I just don't want to lose you in the nerdery of science. We ain't got time for that right now, and if I may recite the famous actor Adam Sandler from his iconic comedy movie about growing up later in

life, "Chlorophyll....more like Borophyll...right?" – Billy
Madison

Oh, and one more thing. You may feel like you are being
offended at some point during our journey together. Can
we just grow up and not be like the rest of the world that
gets so easily offended. No offense is ever given, it can
only ever be taken. From here on out, our hopes are that
we laugh together, we cry together, and we love together.
And if we can do that daily, that is one heckuva day. If we
can learn to do that seven days a week, we are going to
have a special life on our hands. – modified from Jimmy
V's famous Espy speech.

We lied, I guess it wasn't the last thing before we dive in,
because here is one last important thing before we begin,
let me introduce you to my amazing daughter, Livia. I have
already mentioned her a bit above; however, there is a lot
more to her. Livia is my beautiful,
wonderful, and incredibly rare child of God. Now every
child, in my eyes, is a child of God and incredibly rare, but
what makes Livia so rare is a condition that she has. She
has an incredibly rare form of epilepsy, KCNQ2 Epileptic
Encephalopathy, that leaves her quite delayed in most of
the ways a human can be delayed. She cannot walk, yet.
She cannot talk, yet. She cannot hold her head up, yet. She
cannot roll-over, yet. But there is a lot that she can do, and
we focus on that. We bet there are a lot of things that you
perceive that you cannot do, also. Maybe you cannot run
fast, yet. Maybe you cannot talk in front of people, yet.
Maybe you cannot hold your head up high and look people
in the eye, yet. Maybe you cannot take and roll with the
punches thrown at you in life, yet. However, just like Livia,
there is a lot that you can do, and we will focus on that and

23

we will prove that all of your "cannots" are really just imagined inabilities.

1 PATIENCE

This is a tough one for me personally. Admittedly, I am very impatient. I'm driven by results, not only for myself, but more-so for others. I have always been wired that way. So, when results do not come quickly for Livia, my knee-jerk is to get frustrated, and that is a flaw of mine. Livia is teaching me every day, multiple times, that I must learn to be patient with the process, and to learn to control what I can control. When I look back on past successes in my life, I am reminded that most great things happen over a long period of time because of faith and consistency. Liv reminds me that my faith, strength, and unusual peace and confidence about the outcome lies with the Lord above.

One of my favorite quotes is, "God feeds the birds every morning, but he doesn't put the worms in their mouths." This is a great reminder that while we cannot control everything, we are in control of many things, and I for one know that I am not a quitter. I never have been, and I never will be. Livia reminds me that I am in control of that, and she is my daughter born into a family of non-quitters. I think God knew that and said in the Heavens above before she was born, "Brandon and Jenny will have a daughter, a daughter with beautiful challenges that man has yet to fully understand...and through those challenges, that little wonder will teach Brandon and Jenny many lessons, which will then be taught to the masses of people with ears to hear. He continued, but this daughter MUST be born into the family of Brandon and Jenny LaRue, because they possess an uncanny ability to believe and not quit, and this is a lesson that Livia will need most on her life journey."

"So it shall be," His voice thundered, "Livia, the Warrior, shall be born into the Brandon and Jenny LaRue family." Thank you Little Warrior for the first lesson of patience. Daddo promises to model and teach you to always believe and never quit if you promise to keep teaching me your lessons. Deal?

Call me a child of the 90s, but whenever I hear the word *patience*, I immediately think of this:

"I've been walking the streets at night
Just trying to get it right
It's hard to see with so many around
You know I don't like being stuck in the crowd
And the streets don't change but maybe the names
I ain't got time for the game 'cause I need you
Yeah, yeah, yeah but I need you
Oh, I need you
Oh, I need you
Ooh this time."

- *Guns and Roses*

To be honest, I'm not quite sure if that part of the song jives with the content of this book, but let's all face it, that's a pretty sweet song and when Axel busts loose into the lyrics above, we all try to channel our inner "hair nation" and hit them high notes. Am I right? Anyone? Buehler?

Moving on...

What is patience? The dictionary defines it as "the capacity to accept or tolerate delay, trouble, or suffering without getting angry or upset." Patience, what a virtue! The more challenging things get in life the more we need it, but the less we appreciate our need for it. If you are a person that is struggling in your health and perhaps you have put on 50-100lbs of excess weight that you no longer want to be carrying around, well guess what, that is going to require some patience...

Cuz the diets don't change,
but maybe the names,
and you ain't got time for those games,
cuz yo family needs you,
yeah, yeah cuz they need you...
(now hit them high notes) OH, THEY NEED YOU,
OHHHHH, THEY NEED YOU,
OOOOOHHHHH THIS TIME.

I guess the song is relevant after all!
If you are an entrepreneur and you have a vision for what you want to build and what it could be for your family, you must know that nothing great is ever built overnight. So, quit being so delusional in thinking that it

is going to happen quickly or easily. It is going to be hard and it is going to require patience.

Or perhaps you are like Livia and I, praying to God multiple times a day for a miracle to heal her. Maybe you are battling depression, anxiety, cancer, joblessness, unworthiness, or lack of purpose. All of this requires patience in knowing that there is purpose for your life. There is a creator who created you for a very specific reason to do something of immeasurable value that only YOU can do. If we think that this all-important purpose is going to be revealed RIGHT NOW then we feed into the lie from the devil because it most likely won't happen to you right now, and that's when the devil, the one who comes to steal, kill, and destroy, will begin to play his mind tricks. As it says in the Bible in Romans 5:2-4:

> Through whom we have gained access by faith into this grace in which we now stand. And we boast in the hope of the glory of God. Not only so, but we also glory in our sufferings, because we know that suffering produces perseverance; perseverance, character; and character, hope.

By the way, I'm a believer and disciple of Jesus Christ. Are you weirded out yet? If so, good, it is only gonna get weirder. There is profound wisdom in those scriptures above where it states, "suffering produces perseverance; perseverance, character; and character, hope." In other words, nothing worth doing will be easy, nor will it likely come fast. We must have patience.

3: Livia, and her younger sister Bradie, teaching me a valuable lesson in patience.

2 SURRENDER

"The ultimate illusion of the human experience is control. The person you want beside you in the battle is the guy who has surrendered the outcome and has surrendered to the fact that he might die. When you surrender the outcome, you are freed up to be at your best, to be in the moment, and to trust your training. It is the one who has surrendered the outcome who quite honestly has the greatest chance of survival."

— Chop Wood Carry Water by Joshua Medcalf

This is one of the more challenging lessons that Livia has taught me and is now teaching you. We must learn to surrender the outcome. What does that even mean, little girl?

[Through Livia's eyes] "It means that I may never say 'I love you' from my mouth, but I promise you, Daddo, that I'll love you in other ways more important than words. It means that I may never walk, but I promise you, Daddo, that it is okay, because that means you get to carry me longer. It means I may not live as long as "normal" healthy people may live, but quantity doesn't compare to quality of years."

Before we move one, let's address "Daddo." A couple weeks back, a friend of mine asked me when my son, Brooks, called me Daddo, "What's a Daddo?" I laughed and then responded, "When I had kids, I didn't want them to call me what all kids call their fathers. I wanted my 'Dad-name' to be different, just as I wanted to be a different kind of Dad. So, Daddo was born!" So from now on, if you hear me say "Daddo," know that I am referring to myself.

At the core, what this lesson really means is that you cannot control the outcome. It means the only thing you can control is what is happening right now. It means that the worst may happen and being okay with that allows you to experience the now and be ever more present in the moments that matter. Unfortunately, most people just allow the potential outcome to lead to nothing but worry and fear, leaving them debilitated. It means that if all you do is worry about what could happen, you will miss out on all the best moments right in front of your face. It means that we are all mortal bodies with immortal souls.

31

What about death? Whoa. What a concept that we all tend to avoid and then act so surprised when it happens. Guess what the death rate of all humanity is?

What did you guess? Did you guess 100%? If you did, you are certainly very close! The answer is 99.99999999999% and you know who that .00000000000001 person is? His name is Jesus! And what is so great about surrendering the outcome in this scenario is that as believers and disciples of Jesus Christ, we know that we will most certainly die, but in that death, we will rise! We have eternal life in Heaven as the outcome! How freeing and incredible is that?

It is this very promise that allows us to live with peace that transcends all understanding when the storms of life hit us right between the eyes. We know that if the worst thing in this life, death, happens, we get Heaven! I'm telling you, my friend, this is real and I pray your heart is open and not hardened. If you do not have this type of freedom in your life, Livia and I both invite you to ask Him into your heart right now. Don't even second guess it. For it says in the Bible:

> If you confess with your mouth that Jesus is Lord and believe in your heart that God raised him from the dead, you will be saved. For with the heart one believes and is justified, and with the mouth one confesses and is saved (Romans 10: 9-10).

When your eternity is secured, you're able to become a dangerous force for good, and live a life with Holy reckless abandon. The cares of this world don't leave you completely, but they are minimized. The adversity in your life is met with your Holy fists. Your shortcomings become your strengths because you're not alone, you have Christ on your side and He will show up in your weakness. Your addictions, sins, and old ways of thinking can be made anew and completely transformed.

So, surrender the outcomes in your life, but please address this one with the creator of the universe first. Because if you can be at peace and victorious in surrendering that outcome, you'll be able to surrender all other outcomes you're faced with in your life with strength and grace. It's a freedom that is unimaginable, yet so accessible to everyone!

Look, you and I both know that King of Kings and the Lord or Lords has been knocking on your heart for a very long time. You've asked yourself questions like, "Why do I exist? What's my purpose? What happens when we die? Is Heaven for real? How does a 747 really fly!?" Maybe that last question is just me, but every time I'm up in the air on that massive piece of metal with wings and I'm reminded how wonderful our creator is to have created us in His likeness with a fraction of his infinite intelligence and wisdom to be able to construct such a thing! And as the great Andy Stanley says, "If a man can predict his own death and resurrection, and pull it off, I just go with whatever that man says."

Until we learn to surrender outcomes, we will continue to be inundated with the cares and worries of this world, and when we do that, we can't truly live. In other words, it means, "Every man dies, but not every man lives." - *Braveheart*

4: Because we've surrendered the outcome, we can attack each day with a sense of joy, determination, and peace. This can only happen when you've secured the most important thing in life, and that is: What are you going to do with Heaven?

3 WORK

As I hold Livia, just two days from her fourth birthday, I ponder her unique disability. Because her condition is so rare that even some of the brightest neurologists in the world have told us that they learn more about this condition of KCNQ2—a form of epilepsy where her potassium channels in her cells are essentially turned off, leading to an electrolyte dysfunction with motor control—from us as her parents than from what science can tell us right now.

The best way I can understand it is that the human body is so meticulously created that even the slightest thing as an electrolyte dysfunction in one of her genes, can cause so much disruption that she can't hold her head up on her own. She can't bring a finger to scratch an itch on her

35

nose. She can't roll over on her own. It disrupts her cognition where she can't talk. I can't even imagine what type of work and effort it must take for her to do the things that she can do and the work and effort it must take to try to do the things that we all take for granted that we can do.

In our household, we do not allow the word "can't" to be used, and in the paragraph above, I want you to count the amount of times I typed the word "can't." I purposely used that word because that is how most people view difficult tasks and challenges in their life. They focus on the things they tell themselves that they *can't* do rather than focusing on what they can do. Most likely *can't* is really a *won't* for many people, and until they exchange the vowel "O" for an "A" in the word "won't" (and also remove the apostrophe ya wisenheimer) they'll remain stuck simply because they are confusing their vowels!

So, rather on focusing what Livia can't do, we focus on what she can do. She's far better at many things than I, thus all these lessons she is teaching me, and now you, in this book. It doesn't mean that we don't work hard on the things that she struggles with, because obviously we hope she can do those things much better down the road. Just like all of us with our own things that we struggle with that wish we were better at. Shouldn't we all be doing the same? Shouldn't we all work to become more capable of some things that we aren't good at in order to become more proficient? By doing this, we are focusing on what we can do. And boy oh boy, what Livia can do is pretty amazing.

She has the most angelic language that you could ever imagine. Her coos, smiles, and laughs stop anyone dead in their tracks and nearly bring you to tears. She is unable to use what we refer to as words yet her unique language often has me wondering if her way of communication is more advanced than our own. Because man oh man, she can communicate, there's no *can't* in this household. And Livia and I hope to encourage you to remove that word from your vocabulary, as well.

Few things that are great have ever come with ease. Most everything that we admire, be it a 747, a skyscraper, an author of a book □, one of those viral videos of a disabled veteran doing an incredible athletic feat, and even your own journey here towards your personal greatness, will all carry with them a heavy workload. Keep in mind that the work is worthy and worthwhile.

Why do we waste so much time worrying about what other people will think about us? Why do we waste so much time behind our phones scrolling and trolling? Why do we waste time binging on Netflix? We all know how this story ends for us all in this life, and you and I both know this FACT: When we reflect back on our lives, do you really think we will sit there and wish we had worried more about the opinions of others? Do you really think you would have wished you hadn't missed season seven of *Breaking Bad*? Do you think you really wish you would've passed on all those opportunities that crossed your path? Do you really think we will wish we would've done more or less with our lives? If we can begin with the end in mind, we can all learn from this right now and we can begin.

37

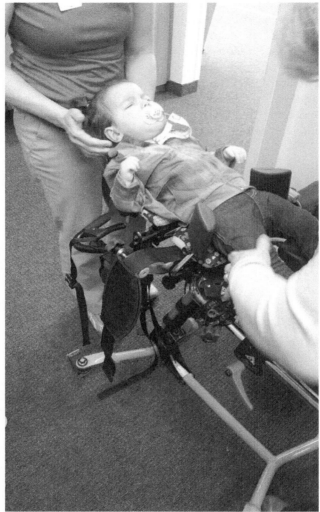

5: Livia getting into her stander for the first time so she can see the world in an upright position. This requires a lot of "work" for her even though she is fully supported.

4 MEDICATION

I'd like to take a moment to give a shout out to the
medical community. You know the ones that sacrifice
years and years and hundreds of thousands of dollars to
pursue the caring of me and you when we are sick and
injured? Yeah, those folks! In today's "enlightened" world
where we are all so smart and wise that we self-diagnose
and self-treat ourselves with the words of wisdom from
Food Babe and the like, let's remember that these folks
probably know a little bit more about the human body,
physiology, biochemistry, and pharmacology than you and
I do. Now this isn't to say that we shouldn't be proactive
with our health and fitness and that we shouldn't do
everything that we do to avoid pharmaceuticals. But ladies
and gentlemen, these medical folks do know a thing or two
because they've seen a thing or two (thanks, Farmer's
Insurance commercials). If it wasn't for modern medicine,
we wouldn't have advanced the average lifespan to the
point it is today. So, let's all be thankful for modern

39

medicine and stop vilifying it like it's the enemy. Is it perfect? Of course not! Are you perfect? Of course not! I have to believe that anyone that is willing to go through that kind of *grueling schooling* and then years and years of residency at the risk of hundreds of thousands of dollars of debt, have a heart to help you and me. Ever been to a children's hospital? There are literally angels on earth walking around those halls. They have a love for your children that almost equals your own.

We witnessed this firsthand the first month of Livia's life when we were in the NICU at the University of Minnesota Children's Hospital. When she was born, she began having episodes that were initially thought of as reflux by the doctors, but on the third day in the hospital as she was being evaluated by a physical therapist, she had an episode. That's when it was realized that it was a seizure rather than reflux…that's when everything changed. She was loaded up into an ambulance and taken to the NICU at the University of Minnesota Children's Hospital where she was carefully evaluated. She was poked and prodded more times that you and I will likely ever be in our lifetime. She was hooked up to an EEG for most of that month, as they evaluated her brain, and she was given anti-seizure medication to lessen the frequency of seizures. We were blessed to find a medication right out of the gate that worked for Livia at a very low dose.

I'm sure my wife would agree, but as a father, once you've seen your child have a seizure and there's nothing you can do about it, you'll gladly allow the breakthroughs of modern medicine to provide an intermediate solution until there's a cure. Enter the lesson from Livia on medication. After a quick Google search, there's a couple definitions of the word *medicine*. "A substance used for medical treatment, especially a medicine or drug," is one definition, and the other "a treatment using drugs." Let's go down a couple paths as we dive deeper into Livia's lesson. The first path is a tough one for most that will read this. Let's dissect the word *drug*. A drug is a chemical substance, typically of a known structure, which, when administered to a living organism (you), produces a biological effect. A pharmaceutical drug, also called a medication or medicine, is a chemical substance used to treat, cure, prevent, or diagnose a disease or to promote well-being. So this begs the question, what drugs are you using? If we use that definition of a drug, do you drink alcohol? That's a drug. Do you smoke? That's a drug. Do you chew tobacco? That's a drug. Do you binge eat? That's a drug. Do you take opioids? That's a drug.

Now some of you may be rolling your eyes with this perspective, but the truth of the matter is that nearly everything we consume is a chemical and produces a biological effect. So we all take a multitude of drugs, some beneficial, some not so much. You've heard it said, "movement is medicine," but are we administering the drug of exercise to produce a positive biological effect for your living organism? You've also heard it said, "You are what you eat." But once again, are you administering good drugs here or bad drugs? How about the type of TV, music, and other media that you inject into your living organism? What are you injecting into your eyes and ears? If you don't think that those substances that we consume produce a biological effect, you're out of touch with reality, and it's a lie from the pits of hell. If you're a woman and you're binging on *Desperate Housewives* or *Fifty Shades* guess what kind of perspective and views you're literally downloading into your mental hardware? Keep

41

administering toxic doses of infidelity, lust, and gossip into your eyes and ears, and guess what could happen? What type of effect is that going to have? If you're a man and you're administering doses of porn and nights out at the strip club with "the boys" (exactly, boys), what type of effect do you think that is having on your living organism? What effect do you think that is going to have on how you view your wife, girlfriend, and the entire female gender? You know it in your soul, right at this very moment, that it's the wrong medication to be injecting into your life.

As you are beginning to realize is that we have control over a lot of the drugs that we get administered in our life, and our choices can severely alter our mind, body, and soul. Let's learn to administer the good stuff. Health and fitness is a great starting point for much of this. As Stephen Covey puts it, "It [health and fitness] has a tremendous spillover effect into all other areas of our lives."

42

5 CHALLENGE

What is it about challenge that causes some to rise up and elevate their game to new heights, while others it strikes fear into their hearts and they cower at the thought of being outside their comfort zone? Speak in front of a crowd of people? Heavens, no! "I'd rather die," is what most people say, and in fact, most people fear public speaking more than they fear death. And how about the business you always wanted to start because you hate working for "the man?" You enjoy dreaming of the day when you'd be able to work for yourself and build something you've always dreamed of building, but what will others think of you? What about that guy or gal that you feel like might be "the one" and have wanted to ask out on a date for a while now. But, what if they say no? How awful would that rejection be?

Look, life is full of challenges, and the few I listed above are just a small offering of the many challenges we all face. We all want greatness in our lives until it's time to do what greatness requires. Greatness comes in many different forms in many different areas of our lives. Personally, I want to be my greatest as a man of faith, a husband, a father, and as an extractor of greatness in the lives of others; however, I know this does not happen without significant challenge. Because nothing great was ever built with ease. It takes a challenge to forge great things.

Livia is a beautiful example and reminder of challenge for me on a daily basis. I can't even fathom what it must be like to desire to move, to walk, to sit upright, and try to coordinate all the simple movements we take for granted. Or the words that I know she wants to form with her voice so she can express herself accurately, but can't. She overcomes that hurdle to express herself in unique coos and facial expressions that anyone who spends time with her can understand so well. Being around her reminds me of how blessed we all are and it also reminds me how challenges are to be embraced, not avoided. They are to build us up, not tear us down; in fact, without a challenge, no growth occurs. Livia reminds me, a strength coach, that if a muscle or bone does not get challenged, they atrophy. When joints and muscles do not move regularly though a range of motion, you tend to lose that freedom of movement, even at four years old. She reminds all of us that we are to treat this one vessel we have with the respect and honor that it deserves and to CHALLENGE it! Not to fuel it with garbage like Doc Brown fuels the flux capacitor in *Back to the Future II* (I may be dating myself here). Our bodies don't work that way. We need to feed it good quality fuel *most* of the time. There's no challenge in Netflix binging and being lazy and wasting

44

your one body away and allowing the atrophy of bone and muscle simply because you're not willing to use it. Move and challenge your body continually.

You know what the report from the other side is about moving and challenging your body and also fueling it with good stuff most of the time is? The report is always, without one exception in my experiences, GREAT! So pursue greatness and be willing to do what greatness requires. It's laid out in this book and we can all be the beneficiaries of little Liv's pursuit towards GREATNESS with her constant challenge that she faces daily.

6 CRIPPLING

This is a lesson Livia that she, and her accomplice, God, dropped on me this morning while getting her ready for school. To allow you into our world a little deeper yet, I was getting ready to shower with her. I can't quite describe how wonderful this experience is for me, as her Dad, but it's one of my favorite times together. If you try to dirty joke that last sentence, I will personally drive to your house and punch you in the face. Just saying.

I'm an athlete at heart and the Lord has blessed me with quite a bit of athleticism, and of all the athletic accomplishments, feats of strength, and future competitions I'll participate in and do well in, nothing will compare to the athletic accomplishment of being able to hold my wonderful, slippery, sudsy, low-muscle-tone daughter in my arms, support her body everywhere that she needs to be supported, balancing her on one of my

46

legs to free up one hand to get the shampoo and body wash out of the bottle and then onto her hair and body to wash her, handing her off from one arm to the next, partially because I need to rinse both sides of her hair and body and also partially because my biceps are on fire, and then my favorite part, sing "Jesus Loves Me" and "I'm Livia, and I'm Wonderful" directly into her ear while she enjoys the warm water on her back.

I'm not crying…I'm sobbing just thinking about it.

So where's this lesson in crippling you ask? Well, here's the lesson she and God taught me right before I even entered the shower with her. What if I didn't take care of myself? What if I was like most Dads who are "too busy" to take care of themselves? What if I didn't have the arm strength, the coordination, the stamina, the flexibility, and the amazing vocal chords—dare I say as smooth as the caramel-y voice of Michael Bublé to sing "Jesus Loves Me" and "I'm Livia, and I'm Wonderful?"

What a crippling existence that must be. And the deeper lesson within it all, how crippling that would be for my children to witness a Dad who was too out of shape to run, jump, play, and *almost* match their energy levels. It's because my six-year-old son sees me carrying Livia everywhere, that he always wants to carry my one-year-old Bradie around everywhere, and he usually does! He even asks if he can carry Livia, and while he can't quite yet, I know that because he sees his Dad do it all the time, that he also wants to be able to lift Livia, as well. A time will come, in the not-too-distant-future, where Brooks will be able to handle Livia as well, and what a sight that will be! It breaks my heart to even think about him not wanting to carry his sisters around simply because Dad was too crippled not to do it himself. It's one thing to be crippled, but it's a whole other thing to willingly be crippled. When I heard that word "crippling" I was instantly reminded of that scene in the movie *Remember the Titans* where Coach Boone, played by Denzel Washington, is having a heated conversation with Coach Yost about the black kids on the team and how Coach Yost was enabling them by protecting them from big bad Boone's disciplinarian approach to coaching. Coach Boone said to Coach Yost, "You ain't doing these kids a favor by patronizing them…you're crippling them…you're crippling them for life."

I know these are tough pills for people to swallow, but I don't want to be like Coach Yost here and stroke any egos, I want to be like Coach Boone.

6: Since this has been written, Brooks has grown strong by doing pullups, pushups, kettlebell swings, goblet squats, sit-ups, sit-outs, box jumps, and other exercises to be able to do be able to carry his sister.

7 CONTROL

I pray hard multiple times a day for my Livia to be healed, and it can'get frustrating if all I do is focus on outcomes. Outcome based goals are a big problem with people and a big flaw with goal setting. Most people do not understand proper goal setting. I was working with an elite 16u hockey team about goal setting recently, and as an experiment I asked each of them to tell me their goals. Can you guess what goals were? "Make it to the NHL or play DI 'cawledge hawkey.'" After they all shared their goals with me, I boldly told them, "You know you have no control over that, right?" They looked perplexed. I told them, "You can't control who's scouting you, how much scholarship money is available, if you'll be playing on the day the scout shows up, if you have a career-altering injury, if a coach doesn't like you, or if there's just someone who

is better than you." I could tell this was some stuff that they had never heard before. I said, "Outcome based goals, which you all shared with me right now, are goals that you really have no control over, and If you can't control the outcome, then what can you control?" The room was silent for a few moments, then one kid piped up and said, "Our actions."
"Exactly," I replied.

You have to learn to control what you can control and embrace the process. This is all too cliché but when you break it down, it's 100% accurate. I took out a whiteboard and a marker and had them begin coming up with habits that would align with the outcome goal of making it to the DI level or the NHL. The ideas came flooding in:

Have a great attitude
Lift weights during the off-season, not just in-season
Eat like an athlete and not like a turd
Get good grades in school
Train the mind as much as I train the body

Now we were getting somewhere...

Now I know, I know; I need to take a dose of my own medicine here, and this is what I've begun to do with my beautiful princess. I need to control what I can control, and I need to embrace the process, just as Livia does. If you know me at all in the slightest, you know that patience is NOT a personality trait you'd use to describe me, but my patience is, in fact, something I can control. So I'm leaning on God and his timing, and not my own, and through it all, the Lord has blessed us with a very special brand of love and a very special relationship that is as rare as her condition. And our way of communication, which is also as rare as she is, is like our own special language that only we get to share together. Nobody else outside of our family and those angels (shout out to all the PTs, OTs, Special Education teachers, babysitters, etc.) who also work with her consistently, will truly get to communicate this way with her. In the meantime, while I pray for the cognitive abilities so that she can use words instead of coos, I get to experience moments like this, and then the Holy Spirit speaks to me loud and clear:

https://www.youtube.com/watch?v=Gx6caAONh6o&t=21s

"She is speaking to you DADDO!"

Therein lies the lesson from Livia. With the language of love, words aren't always necessary, and if we just learn to embrace the process and control what we can control, all with the smile and wonder that radiates from Livia, we will put ourselves in positions to experience the outcome we're praying for.

I'm so grateful for you and these lessons you teach me, little girl. And I'm so grateful for the Lord's blessings on your life and how rare our relationship is. It also reminds me of how grateful I am for my relationship with Jesus. The peace and strength He gives me during the storms of life are real.

Until the day comes when I hear the word "Daddo" come out of your mouth, honey, I will praise the Lord for all of our rareness together.

8 SERIAL CASTING

It happened yet again. Livia was just going around being beautiful, wonderful, and tough when she delivered another lesson for me, and hopefully, all of us. Livia's condition leads to some less than desirable dystonia (muscular balance, function, coordination) and some of her limbs aren't growing correctly due to the dystonia. Her lower legs, particularly her ankles, have inverted toward the midline of her body, and if something isn't done to correct it, they will continue to grow incorrectly than the ankles are intended. So the doctors have decided to do serial casting on her lower legs to course correct this. Before the serial casting is done, they inject her lower legs with botox to basically paralyze her overactive muscles that are leading to the malalignment of her ankle. The best way I can describe serial casting is that it's a lot like braces for your teeth. Slowly, consistently, and gradually, the casting is designed to progressively manipulate her ankles into alignment. She giggled when she got the botox injections by the way; she truly is a tough little girl; that's not just her Daddo talking. What's quite interesting is how ingrained her dystonia is, because when you take her cast off just for a few minutes in order to put on the new progressive cast, you can tell how her ankles want to continue to go back to their old ways.

And that's where it happened. I realized the lesson she was teaching me. She was showing me that a limb can grow incorrectly due to the pressures placed upon it, but it's only just a limb. What about a life? How maladjusted can we all become when we give into the pressures that are placed upon us? How far off track can our lives get when for weeks, months, years, and even decades we give into peer pressure? How about when we give into the pressures of an addiction? How far off track does it take us from our destiny? What about soaking in a sea of negativity? Like the botox in Livia's legs paralyzing her muscles, how does that negativity paralyze your belief, hopes, and dreams? Or what about the pressures of the world? Are you succumbing to what it wants for you? It says in Romans 12:2, which I refer to often, "Do not conform to the patterns of this world, but be transformed by the renewing of your mind." If we were to look at how God views us, and how the world views us as a painting of ourselves, I envision the one the world paints us all conformed and distorted, like a Picasso painting. The distortion in the painting is only a metaphor for how altered our values, character, and destiny have become. Then there's the painting God does of us. I think it scares most people to even ask the question, "What would God's painting of me look like?" Personally, I think you'd be speechless at the beauty, perfection, and love you'd see in the strokes of that paintbrush.

54

I think what Livia, and the Lord Almighty, are trying to teach us, is to allow Him to be our serial casting. Allow Him to ever so slightly, consistently, and gradually, mold us into our ideal self and our ideal destiny. Let Him sift

through our heart and mind like botox, paralyzing the overactive muscles of self-pity, bitterness, rage, anger, slander, and envy. Ultimately, allow Him to correct you and make a painting of your life so wonderful and so magnificent; and then allow Him to put his autograph on that painting. He created you after all.

Whoa.

All that from your beautiful, crooked little ankle, Livia? You amaze me, and you're the closest thing to Heaven on this side of the story for this father of yours. How did you get so smart!?

7: Livia sporting her cast as she takes a sweet nap on the Mississippi River.

9 FASCINATION

"Turn your frustration into fascination." I'm not sure if this was an original phrase that my friend JP told me one time, or if he heard it from somewhere else. It doesn't really matter who said it first, I just know that he was the first to say it to me. It was said in regards to a business that we were involved in together. Human beings are so awesome, but they can also be very frustrating to work with. Say one thing, but do another. Walk right up the starting line, only to back away, time after time after time. Irrational fears that hold them back from greatness in their lives. These types of things when working with people used to drive me bananas. I'd call my mentor up to vent a little bit and he'd usually just chuckle a little bit because he'd been there before and had already learned this lesson. He'd just say, "Brandon, learn to be fascinated by it all."

"Fascinated!?" I responded with obvious irritation in my voice."
What he was trying to get me to do was to look at it from a different perspective, and truth be told, I needed a better perspective.

Being frustrated with people, although I would rarely express that to the person, costs a lot of energy, and frustration is negative energy. Furthermore, it doesn't help the perspective or light in which you are seeing that person. If you're frustrated with them, it'll be more difficult to help them. We all need less frustration in our life, so learning to be fascinated by people rather than frustrated is pure wisdom. It not only lessens the negative energy, but it allows you to see people in the right light. Not as people with shortcomings, but as people who need encouragement and perspective themselves. This changes everything.

The person who best puts this into action is my daughter, Livia. When I fall short in this area, like noticeably losing my patience or getting frustrated with her, whether it be feeding her or changing her clothes, you know what she does? She graces me with her patience and I know she is just fascinated with me. I can just see her thinking in her brain, "Daddo, don't you think if I was able, I would cooperate better? Do you think that I want to make eating and getting dressed difficult on myself?" Boy oh boy does the shift in perspective change everything. Why was I the one getting frustrated? If anyone should be frustrated, and rightfully so, it should be Livia! So, while this lesson was verbalized by one of my best friends, it is executed beautifully by none other than my beautiful daughter, Livia. Thank you for your grace and patience, little girl.

And thank you, thank you, thank you for being fascinated, not frustrated, with your goofy Dad who's trying to learn all these lessons you're teaching.

8: When I learned to be fascinated, rather than frustrated, it began to change my demeanor about all the challenges that Livia and I face together.

10 LISTEN

You know how they say, "You have two ears and one mouth, so we should listen twice as much as we speak?" We've all heard it before, but few put it into practice. Most people do the opposite. They hear, but they are only looking for their next opportunity to talk, while there are others who only talk, never giving themselves a chance to even listen. There are even several verses in the Bible in the book of Proverbs covering this practical piece of life wisdom:

Proverbs 10:17 "People who accept correction are on the pathway to life, but those who ignore it will lead others astray."
Proverbs 13:1 "A wise child accepts a parent's discipline; a young mocker refuses to listen.
Proverbs 13:13 "People who despise advice will find themselves in trouble; those who respect it will succeed."

Proverbs 15:22 "Plans go wrong for lack of advice; many counselors bring success."
Proverbs 16:20 "If you reject criticism, you only harm yourself; but if you listen to correction, you grow in understanding.
Proverbs 16:20 "Those who listen to instruction will prosper; those who trust the Lord will be happy."
Proverbs 19:20 "Get all the advice and instruction you can, and be wise the rest of your life."
Proverbs 19:27 "If you stop listening to instruction, my child, you have turned your back on knowledge."
Proverbs 23:12 "Commit yourself to instructions; attune your ears to hear words of knowledge."

You may not be aware of this, but the Book of Proverbs is widely considered one of the most profound and practical collections of wisdoms ever assembled. From the youngster to the experienced, the wisdom is timeless and never ending. Therefore, I think the point is made that listening is an important skill to develop and learn.

No one that I've ever met in my life demonstrates this more than Livia. She's always listening and keenly aware of what's going on around her. She doesn't try to overpower you with her voice, like many try to do when they think their point of opinion is more important than yours. She chimes in with her beautiful coos, smiles, and smiling eyes when the mood and circumstances are appropriate, otherwise, she just listens. There are times she is so quiet and just taking it all in that I forget that she's right next to me or in the next room. She rarely ever begs for attention unless she needs it, and she loves being in the thick of the commotion and mixing it up with people. It's a remarkable lesson to learn from her in how powerful spoken words are to those who are listening. I'm just a flawed Dad doing

61

my best to be more like Jesus, so I slip up and make mistakes. I lose my temper sometimes. I get impatient. I say things that I wish I could take back as soon as the words exit my mouth. And guess who doesn't miss a thing because she's always listening? Livia. Her temperament changes on a dime when my mood and attitude take a dive. Conversely, when I'm speaking words of encouragement, love, and prayers over her, she beams with smiles and glows with love. How can someone who listens nearly 90% of the time, make such an impact on others? The answer lies within the question; she listens.

11 ATROPHY

The definition of the word atrophy is *"gradually decline in effectiveness or vigor due to underuse or neglect."* Generally speaking, when we think of the word *atrophy* we think of it in relation to our bodies and how they decline from underuse or the aging process. With your average four-year-old, the last thing you typically have to wonder about is atrophy occurring due to underuse. I mean my goodness, you'd think they are all on a continuous IV drip of caffeine to maintain that type of energy throughout their days! I'm experiencing this with my six-year-old son and my 18-month-old daughter as I type. It's like they have lightning bolts running through their veins!

This is not the case with my little warrior princess, Livia. Her lack of muscle tone and motor control leaves her non weight-bearing most of the day. She lays, she sits in her wheelchair, and we are working towards getting her in her stander more as she builds up tolerance for being upright

63

while bearing weight in her uncomfortable ankle foot orthotics (AFOs). Because of this lack of use, and the lack of stress applied to her body, she's got the most beautiful little chicken legs and arms. I long for those muscles to be more supple, strong, and filled out, but there's a lesson she's teaching us with those little chicken limbs. She's reminding us to use ours, BECAUSE WE CAN! She is a constant reminder that we should be grateful for the little things, from being able to pick our own nose to being able to throw some weight on our back and be able to squat without pain.

She also reminds us about other aspects of our lives that gradually decline in effectiveness or vigor due to underuse or neglect. How about our marriages? Gulp. How about the depth and breadth of our skills? How about our faith? This list could go on and on, but outside of our muscles and bones atrophying, why are so many people atrophying in their marriages? Shouldn't there be a respectable increase in the amount of intimacy and romance present in our marriages? Shouldn't we all be getting smarter, thinking better, developing more skills, and making a larger impact? And shouldn't we be growing closer, stronger, and more bold in our spiritual life?

You see, most people think that experience equates to the amount of time that has passed. To be very frank, it doesn't. If you were ever in a worker's union, perhaps you grew up with the "seniority thing" and the entitlement that came from just existing in one place long enough. Unions are a good thing, in theory, until our humanness decides to take part. Anyone who was ever in a worker's union knows what I'm talking about. Experience doesn't happen with time. Experience happens with a plan for growth and then taking action upon that plan. The acquisition of knowledge isn't much better unless that knowledge is applied.

Knowledge without application is powerless. A person is no better off having the knowledge and not using it than the person who doesn't possess the knowledge in the first place. You could also argue that at least the unknowing person isn't being hypocritical, they just don't know any better.

The lesson Livia is teaching us all is that we must be intentional about our growth plan in life and not just be bystanders expecting to get ever-increasing wages or benefits in life due to us standing around and just accruing time. She's telling us to use our bodies, minds, and souls to ever-increasing amounts so that we don't atrophy. That way our relationships are richer, our impact on others is greater, and we end up on the right side of eternity. Man, I love those little chicken limbs of hers.

12 STARE

I remember back in college there was this long walk to the strength and conditioning room at Minnesota State University – Mankato. So, in this long hallway, you'd always see a bunch of fellow athletes navigating their way from the fieldhouse or class to the weight room. As a young college male, full of testosterone, I found myself checking out the beauty all around me often, if you're picking up what I'm putting down. If you've ever hunted whitetail deer before and saw a younger two-year-old buck running around all clumsy, grunting and checking out every female in the vicinity, yeah, I was that guy. Thank God for his grace on my actions during those years. Of all that looking I did, I don't remember hardly any of it, except for the fact that I did it; but I do remember this one instance quite vividly, where I was staring at something beautiful.

I remember these nice, supple, voluptuous...calves. Easy there Horny Henry, keep it in your pants. I know where your mind was going with that. Okay, okay Henry, I'll indulge your little fantasy. She had those also, but those calves captivated my 21-year-old mind. Those beautiful, muscular calves busting out of the bottom of the cut sweatpants she was wearing had caught my attention in a big way. I remember thinking to myself, "Dang, check out those beauties!" Of course then follows the next question, "Who is that girl, I don't think I've met her before." Long story short, that girl is now my bride and the woman of my dreams!

Have you ever seen or experienced a person, place, or thing that just captivated every fiber of you? I remember early in my faith walk I read the book *Heaven is for Real*. This is a story about a Pastor's son, Colton Burpo, who undergoes emergency surgery and has a miraculous and irrefutable encounter with Jesus and Heaven. Some of the vivid memories that little boy had of Christ and his experience in Heaven moved me in a big way. I remember wiping tears from my eyes as I read that book. At the end of the book, Colton's father, the author, finally reveals this image, which was painted by a young girl, Akiane Kramarik, who lived halfway across the world. She was being featured on TV for her magnificent piece of artwork of Jesus when little Colton saw the painting on the TV and quickly exclaims, "That's Him!"

Goosebumps. I just stared at this image, and He just stared right back at me. It's beautiful, it's captivating, and it's just...perfect.

This isn't the first time this has happened, however. This is where Livia's lesson was dropped on me. It's kind of crazy how this happens when one of her lessons is bestowed upon her goofy Dad. It's like time slows for a moment as the lesson is happening. Livia and I had just gotten off the

67

elevator and had wheeled her to her school locker and had begun to get her winter jacket, blanket, and stocking cap off. There was this young boy that was standing right next to Livia, and he was just staring at her. Like I said before, this isn't anything new that we haven't yet experienced. It happens with adults quite often, too. As this little boy was staring a Livia, his Mom was across on the other side of the hallway, whispering loudly, "Jonny, quit staring." Jonny kept on staring, captivated in wonder of Livia. "Jonny, quit staring!" She whispered, more sternly. Jonny kept staring. Was it that Livia was in a wheelchair? Was it that she was wearing these super cool braces on her ankles? Was it her beauty? "Jonny!" She said this time without a whisper, and little Jonny finally snapped back to reality and went over to his Mom. I listened covertly to their next exchange and how Mom was explaining to little Jonny that it was rude to stare. I totally understand what her intent is and that she means well, so please don't misunderstand what I'm about to share about Livia's lesson. But, is it rude to stare? When you see something that captivates you, do you stare? When you see someone or something that is different than all of the rest, do you stare? When you see something beautiful, do you stare?

I stare at Livia all the time, and I find her staring at things and staring off into what I refer to as "La La Land," but in my heart I often wonder, is she having visions like that little girl that paints these amazing visions she has, or in her own uniqueness and special strength is she able to experience visions of Heaven that us "normal" folks don't have the ability to experience? Is that only bestowed to my lovely Livia?

So what Livia is trying to get across to us all is this; it's okay to stare at things in wonder, in reverence, and in love. But I think Livia would like us all to take it one step

68

further than the stare. She'd like us to take action and approach what it is we are staring at. If it's a boy or girl that has captivated your attention, go get to know that person and ask them to hang out sometime. If it's Livia, approach her and talk to her. She may respond differently, but she hears every word you say and you'll see those big brown eyes light up, and if you're lucky enough to have those eyes connect with yours, she'll imprint on your soul…it's magical. If it's Jesus knocking on the door of your heart, I think she'd tell us all to open up the door and begin having a conversation with Him.

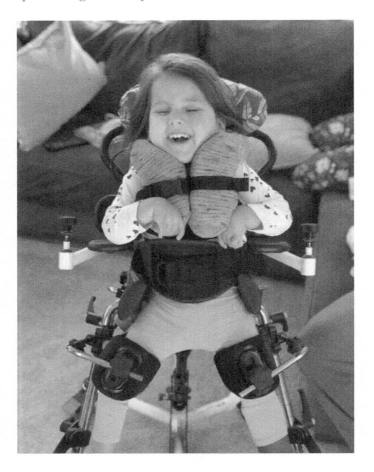

9: It's okay to stare at things that are different, unique, and beautiful, but take one more step and get to know the person or thing that you're staring at.

13 SUPERCOMPENSATION

In sports science theory, supercompensation is the post-training period during which the trained function/parameter has a higher performance capacity than it did prior to the training period. The human body is truly a fascinating creation. Can you just imagine the elaborate design work or blueprint, if you will, that God had of the human body before He created it? Just look at the intricacy of the human eye for example. Or how about that nobody in the world has the same fingerprint as you!? Isn't that wild!? I find it even crazier that some people believe that all of that just happened by "chance."

What I find even more fascinating is how the body changes when resistance is applied to it. Perhaps that's just the strength coach in me, but the plasticity and adaptability of the human body is very much like that of a transformer. Forgive me, I have a son that is enthralled by transformers, namely Optimus Prime, Shockwave, Grimlock, and Bumblebee. These toys were cool when I was his age, so I

71

understand the fascination with them for a youngster. Their ability to transform from a car to a robot, or a plane to a robot is pretty cool, regardless of your age. Physiologically speaking though, when the body is systematically stressed, like in the instance of a dumbbell bicep curl, it forces the arm to grow. The bicep is damaged at the cellular level, and with adequate nutrition, the body literally rebuilds itself up stronger. This phenomenon is known as supercompensation. Sounds a bit like a transformer, right!?

Personally, when I lift weights, I think of it as building armor around my body. I'm building my body to not only be stronger, but I'm also building it with armor to protect it and make it more capable. Livia, as beautiful as she is, has little chicken legs and arms due to atrophy. It's kind of crazy that a little girl could have muscle and bone atrophy at such a young age. But due to lack of motor control, it's very difficult to have the stress systematically applied to her body in order to keep her muscles growing and developing appropriately. So, what we do is aim to keep her joints and muscles flexible and pliable in expectation for the miracle that she will be able to use them on her own one day. But here is the lesson Livia wants us all to realize from her atrophy; she wants us to focus on our ability to create supercompensation in life. She wants us to realize that supercompensation's application isn't just relegated to our body. But it is far more reaching to other areas of our life. Skills can supercompensate. Belief can supercompensate. Comfort zones can supercompensate. Dreams can supercompensate. Compassion can supercompensate. Even love can supercompensate. The secret to allowing this to happen is to continue to stress these areas to force them to grow and to expand.

Fear is the only thing that seems to grow for most people because of the stress that is applied to it constantly. I grew up watching action hero movies with my Dad and brother and there's this one scene from *Conan the Barbarian* that comes to mind when I think about supercompensation. Remember that scene when he's pushing the "Wheel of Pain" as a young boy, then it shows the passing of time as he is coming of age into a man. He goes from being a young boy to a ripped Arnold Schwarzenegger in his prime. Here's the video if you're not sure what I'm talking about:
https://www.youtube.com/watch?v=z5KYZ74OAak

This is as good of a metaphor as any when it comes to something growing when you consistently apply pressure and stress towards something. This can be a force for good, but it can also work against you. If there is one thing you want in your life to do the opposite of supercompensate, or atrophy, it is fear. This is a tricky process, because in order for fear to atrophy, we have to face it in small doses to eradicate it. Just like we need to be exposed to a virus via vaccination so our body can build up the antibodies to fight the virus, we must also expose ourselves to fear in small doses to build up the resilience to the fear itself. This may sound like a conundrum, but what is really happening here is we are systematically applying stress and supercompensating with the faith element in our lives while systematically reducing the stress (atrophying) applied to the fear.

You see, if we just do nothing about our fears and continue to avoid things that we are fearful of, then we are stealing away our brighter future. When we do that, we are subconsciously always feeding and stressing the fear muscle to be ever-present and strong in our lives. We must learn to stress the right thing, and that is faith! We must

stress our comfort zones for our faith to
supercompensate.

Does the thought of public speaking make your skin crawl
with fear? Then guess what you need to do? You need to
expose yourself to public speaking in small doses. That
may start with raising your hand and asking a question in a
small group. One thing I have learned to love about Livia
is she doesn't care who's around her or even what's going
on around her, if she wants to make herself known, she is
going to do so. I envy that about her. She does not
concern herself with what you may think of her if she
begins to cry in a public place. She does not care what you
think if she laughs while everyone is being quiet. She does
not care even if you hear her fart. LOL! Heck, it even
startles her sometimes and it creates quite the humorous
fart-startled giggle. Now I don't think she is suggesting a
complete lack of manners here, it's just her way of
injecting some humor.

In summary, I think what Livia is trying to teach us here is
that we must stress the right areas in our lives and not the
wrong areas. If we want our compassion to grow, then we
must stress serving others. If we want to be healthier
physically, then we must stress our bodies through
resistance and stress the eating of good, quality nutrition.
If we want to grow professionally in our careers, then we
must stress personal development, learning new skills, and
the expansion of our comfort zones. Most importantly, if
we want to love more, we must stress the action of love
towards others. Have you ever found yourself having
difficulty allowing the words, "I love you" or "I'm proud
of you" slip out of your mouth? Whether it's towards a
spouse, a friend, or your own children, begin stressing the
action of actually saying it and showing it. As much as we
all like to think people understand our good intentions,

they do not. What others will surely understand is when you take action with love in your words and deeds.

Once again little girl, you continue to teach your Daddo things about life that are far beyond your years. You are so smart and so strong in many ways that I am not. I am looking forward to supercompensating in all the right ways!

.

14 COMMUNICATION

As a man, our gender typically has a general stigma of
having a lack of good communication. We may hear, but
we don't listen, and we may talk, but we don't always
communicate. I know when having conversations with my
beautiful bride, I sometimes make the mistake of talking at
her while not necessarily communicating with her. This is
something that I'm working to get better at. As a business
leader and coach, I've been complimented on my ability to
communicate a message well, which is very humbling for
me, because that was never a strong suit for me, it used to
be a fear and a weakness.

I remember being a three-sport captain in high school, and
while I believe I led well with my actions, I wasn't a very
good vocal leader. I distinctly remember several times
where I was called upon to say a word of inspiration
during a team huddle or before a big game, and that

typically fell apart on me. A few of the guys would poke fun at me, all in good fun, but I actually became self-conscious of this later in life. If you have a fear of public speaking, or speaking up at all for that matter, you'll be able to relate to this story.

I was a young manager of an exclusive personal training studio in Minnesota back in 2008 when the owner, Clinton Helget, asked me if I wanted to go speak about health and fitness at a local women's networking event. I swallowed hard and said "yes." He said, "It would be good experience and marketing for the studio," as I recall it. Thankfully, Clinton accompanied me to this event to help me out. The plan was for me to take the first part of the presentation and he would take the second half. Clinton ended up doing 99% of that presentation. I froze in front of what seems like thousands of women, which was only a few dozen if my memory serves me correctly, and I couldn't recall a single thing that I had planned to talk about. I looked over at Clinton and said, "Dude, I got nothing." He saw the fear and disappointment in my eyes and took over without a hiccup. Clinton was right, "This was a good experience."

Good thing for me, I'm not a quitter, and when I'm not good at something right away, it actually motivates me to want to get better at whatever it is. It's crazy, people actually look for me to speak at various events nowadays because they think I'm a good communicator and engage the audience well. Just because you are not good at something in the beginning doesn't mean you can't become good at it later. In fact, people can become good or great at just about anything with hard work and consistent effort.

So, at this point in the lesson, you may be asking yourself, what does this have to do with Livia? Just when I thought I was getting pretty proficient at communication, Livia was now becoming a little girl. She was no longer a baby. This was tough for me, because Livia felt like my baby girl for much longer than your average daughter. To this day, I still carry her like a baby and she's almost five. As much as I hope and pray that she doesn't need her Daddo to carry her like this, I cherish every chance I get to hold her in my arms, balance her head on my shoulder, and oh so carefully wash her body and hair while holding her in the shower.

Livia can't communicate with her words like other little girls her age. She uses various coos, cries, and when you're lucky, laughter, which praise God is occurring more frequently with each passing week. I can't quite describe it in words, you just have to see it. I'm quite certain it could cleanse all humanity of evil if they could just witness Livia's smile and laughter. As she was growing into a little girl who was struggling to communicate with her family, I probably struggled the most with communicating with her. Here I was, challenged all over again in a different form of communication. I found my patience run thin at times, and when I couldn't figure out what Livia wanted when she burst into tears (and some quite impressive high notes in her screeches), I would lose my temper and yell. I want everyone to know who reads this, that these were probably the lowest moments of my life, and it had nothing to do with Livia. It had everything to do with me and my lack of patience, lack of compassion, and just pure frustration. This happened a couple of times, and I remember being so disgusted with myself afterwards. How could a Dad of a special needs child lose his temper with the most precious thing in his life? The last time it happened, I hit my knees and cried out to God, literally, "Lord help me and forgive me. I'm struggling here and I need you to intercede. I need your love, forgiveness, wisdom, and guidance to be what this little girl needs." I remember the Lord answering my prayer while watching Jenny handle those same situations with Livia with grace, love, and patience.

Sometimes as men, our pride is our worst enemy. Here was my wife, modeling exactly how to handle this situation right in front of me, like she had done so many times before. The answer to my prayer was Jenny. I don't tell her this enough, but she truly is the most amazing mother. So I learned to communicate with Livia like Jenny does. With that same grace, love, and patience, Livia and I have grown our communication to be quite something. We have all sorts of cooing conversations, I can make her laugh almost on cue now, and we even sing together. Throughout this journey of learning to communicate better with Livia, I've learned how important body language, tone, and patience is to the quality of your communication. If Livia can sense even the slightest frustration with me, it amplifies her emotions. As soon as I remind myself to be patient and have grace, her emotions follow. It's such a powerful lesson for all of us when we communicate with others. Livia was trying to tell me all along, I just wasn't listening. Just watch Momma!

There's no one that can convince me otherwise, that Livia is well aware and understands more than we will ever know. When I pray over her and communicate words of love, encouragement, and gratitude over her, her beautiful brown eyes open wide, and she beams with smiles and coos. When I lost my patience in the past, grew frustrated, and raised my voice, she cried and screamed unrelentingly.

If we don't all take a lesson here from what Livia is trying to teach us about communication, we can ruin relationships. Livia is an isolated case of what is happening internally with others when we communicate correctly. Thank you, Livia, for another one of your life-altering lessons, and thanks to your Mother for figuring it out way sooner than I, so she could lead us to the beautiful communication we now have together.

10: Momma leading the way with grace, patience, and beauty. I've learned so much from her on how to be a better father for Livia.

15 EMPATHY

It's been said that I lack empathy and could use a little more compassion. That's probably true. But like all things, there's a continuum, or a scale, if you will, of any quality. Too much of it and it can be detrimental, too little of it, and it can also be a negative quality. As a self-proclaimed "excuse expert," I tend to lack empathy on certain things because I truly believe people can change and are very capable of overcoming incredible setbacks and undesirable circumstances in their lives. In many instances, the answer to one's plight is right in front of them and they just need someone bold enough to tell them the truth with tough love. However, understanding the other person's perspective and how they see the world can really be vital information in helping them with the change process. After all, how someone views the world impacts how they feel about the world, which ultimately determines their actions. So, I'm learning that empathy is an absolute must.

Guess who my teacher is on this topic? You guessed it, Livia.

By definition, empathy is the ability to understand and share the feelings of another. Livia presents to me a real challenge to truly understand and share her feelings. But through our unique communication style and intimate father-daughter relationship, I believe I'm developing an understanding of her feelings and even share them with her. Much of this was learned via trial and error initially, but as I've just spent quality time with her, talked to her, spoke words of encouragement to her, and witnessed how she handles uncomfortable situations and adversity in her life, I am truly beginning to understand the wonder that is Livia Jean LaRue.

In today's world, there are these egocentric trends and movements of "I do what I want" and "I don't care what you think of me." Isn't that the exact opposite of empathy? If we are to aim to understand others and share their feelings, wouldn't we have to remove or at least reduce our egocentric minds and motives? Wouldn't true empathy revolve around doing good things that positively impact others rather than just doing what you want? Wouldn't true empathy involve caring what others think of us because we possess the ability to influence them either positively or negatively?

I think Livia understands empathy better than anyone I've ever met in my life. She doesn't judge or discriminate. She will take you as you come and just listen and love on you. Yet when you see her circumstances, she reveals something inside of you that hasn't been "called out" in

83

awhile. Oftentimes, it's your excuses, because just spending time with her has the tendency to shift your perspective. Prior to hanging with Ms. Livia, you tend to see the world through your egocentric worldview. You see your excuses as relevant and real. You've acknowledged them for so long that you've built this steely, reinforced wall further entrapping yourself in your prison of excuses. But when your perspective shifts, all of the sudden you begin to see cracks and light shining through the reinforced walls of your excuses. You begin to see that they aren't as impenetrable as you once thought. You see this wonderful little girl who struggles with any deliberate movement of her body, you see that she struggles eating solid food and relies on mostly a liquid diet. You see how she struggles to communicate. What you see is a constant state of struggle with Livia, but what is rare about it is her joy, love, and peace amongst her struggle. Then, you begin to think of your own constant state of struggle and begin to realize that the excuses that have entrapped you are really just brittle little toothpicks by comparison. By empathizing with Livia, we learn that there is joy and peace amongst the struggle, and we learn that we can conquer our excuses because we possess the attributes to do so. We realize that if the beautifully disabled Livia can do it, then we can overcome and conquer our own beautifully disabled selves.

16 NOURISHMENT

I've been passionate about fitness since I was 13 years old. Initially, my interest was to gain a competitive edge on the field of play. I remember when I entered seventh grade as a wrestler. It was a humbling experience. Wrestling has a way of humbling every participant, and it's a big reason I'm such a proponent of the sport. Up through sixth grade, I didn't lose very much. I won most tournaments that I entered, so I kind of thought that would continue to be the norm. Until seventh grade.

You see, in seventh grade, at least in my town and state anyway, you could be wrestling kids that were two or three years older than you and much stronger and more experienced. I went from being what I thought was a pretty dominant wrestler, to a .500 wrestler. After that season, I started to lift weights at home, and by weights I mean I would curl the magazine rack, do calf raises on the

85

stairs, do pushups on the floor, and sit-ups with my legs on the couch. I didn't really know what I was doing, but my Dad did! He took notice in my obvious interest in wanting to get stronger and bought me a sand-filled weight set with a bench that had a leg extension attachment. He showed me a thing or two and I was on my way. Occasionally, Dad would let me tag along to the Flex House Gym in La Crosse, Wisconsin with him, where I'd get to see some big weights get pushed around. I can't say I really followed a training plan, but I was consistent and I got much stronger. That next season, I became the strong kid and began dominating the competition again.

After my first interest in fitness, to gain a competitive edge, then came an interest in gaining a competitive edge with the opposite sex. Call it vanity or whatever, but having a strong, fit body gave me confidence in this area, and I think most would have to agree that it would also help you with confidence in that area, as well. Whatever the case may be, during that time in my life, it's what drove me to continue to workout. After that came college sports, and then…what's after college sports? Thankfully, I found a position in the health and fitness field as a personal trainer, because if there's one thing I'm not, it's a hypocrite. I couldn't coach people how to be healthy and fit and not do it myself. It was wrong at every level, although some people will argue that, and I just can't associate with those folks.

It was around this time that my boss, and now one of my best friends, Clinton Helget challenged me to do a bodybuilding competition. He used my wrestling psyche against me and reverse psychologized me by saying, "You probably couldn't do it." My response was something to the effect of, "Watch me!" Of all the nutrition-related courses that I aced in college, I still didn't really understand it. I would say that's the same for most people who think they understand nutrition because they took a "college course." Can we be honest about most of our college experiences? It was an expensive party for most people, and as long as you showed up to class, did the homework, and passed the tests, you got a piece of paper saying you were legit. In my opinion, and there are exceptions to this, that Bachelor's degree is just an expensive piece of paper. I share that to explain my next point— I didn't begin to understand nutrition and how it interacted with your physiology and body composition until Clinton guided me through this competition. Do you have to go through that to understand nutrition? Absolutely not, this is just part of my journey and how I grew to have a passion for nutrition and how it impacts the body.When applied intelligently alongside a fitness program, it can absolutely transform a body and a life. That passion has never left me, so I've continued to share and teach others how they can understand nutrition and transform their lives by developing a healthy relationship with food and fitness. I say this with truth in love, nobody is living their best lives willingly being overweight, tired, and masking stress and anxiety with eating.

And then comes the wonderful blessing of Livia into my life. Almost from the day she was born, Livia has been on some form of supplemental nutrition. While she was in NICU for the first month of her life, Livia was nourished by a supplemental nutrition solution via vein called TPN (Total Parental Nutrition), which is a profound nutritional discovery by Dr. Stanley Dudrick in the 1960s. This has likely impacted your life or someone in your family tree in some fashion. In fact, if it wasn't for TPN, there's a good chance your family tree wouldn't look the way it does now. You picking up what I'm putting down in that previous sentence? Just in case that one flew over your head, what I'm saying is that some people would have never made it past their first weeks of life if it wasn't for TPN. Livia also lacked the muscular coordination and stamina to nurse from Jenny, so she has been bottle-fed her entire life. She does occasionally eat some food pouches and other things so long as it's an oatmeal-like texture, but most of her nutrition still comes from liquid nutrition. Is it ideal? Heavens, no! But what's fascinating is how she has grown and stayed remarkably healthy, despite her disability. With appropriate perspective and education on supplements, there should be a massive amount of respect for them, and not a general scorn for their use. I believe good food habits combined with quality supplementation is the future for optimal nutrition for all humans.

Livia is now almost five years old and we made the tough parental decision to get her a feeding tube that goes directly into her stomach. Again, ideal? No. But we are oh so grateful for medical advancements that allow for instances such as Livia's. We can now give her the medication she needs, as well as water! Yes, water's consistency is too thin, so the only water Livia has ever ingested was in the form of milk, formula, or Pediasure, but now she can get high quality H_2O delivered directly to her body! Throughout this feeding tube experience, which is very fresh for me because it's still only a few weeks old as I type this, Livia has taught me another lesson about nourishment. Once again, it takes a perspective shift, but I would encourage you to put on a new set of lenses to capture this lesson. If you didn't have the ability to chew and eat food, or drink a liquid with the thinness of water, what would you put in your feeding tube to nourish yourself? Remember, you can't taste it, it's just going directly into your stomach to nourish your body to be healthy, hydrated, and able. Would you put Doritos, Mountain Dew, and Coors Light into a blender and then inject that into your feeding tube still? My guess is that if you bypassed the mouth, you'd probably pick better things to nourish your body. My guess is you wouldn't choose milkshakes and candy bars, and you'd choose a solution jam-packed with nutrient dense calories loaded with vitamins, minerals, amino acids, immune-boosting antioxidants, and other energizing ingredients so you could live your best life.

Thankfully, most of us get to experience the blessing of tasting, chewing, and swallowing our food and beverages. However, this blessing has become a curse for many with over 70% of Americans being overweight or obese and an ever-climbing childhood obesity rate that has soared to over 30%. Take this lesson from Livia to heart. Learn to nourish your body first, and not just satisfy your mouth. Believe it or not, you will learn how to satisfy your mouth in the process of nourishing your body.

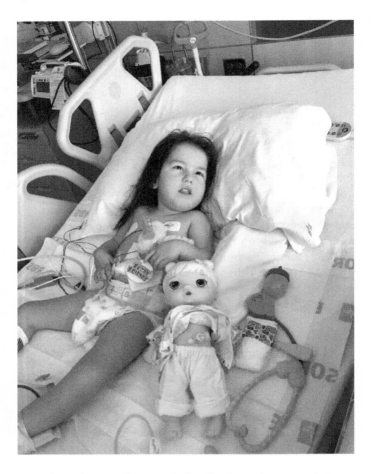

11: Livia coming out of surgery for her G-tube so she can get better nourishment for her growing mind, body, and spirit.

17 ENEMY

Most humans are their own worst enemies. Most of you are shaking your head in agreement right now because you're thinking to yourself, "I know I'm my own worst enemy." We know what is right, yet we often do what is wrong. We know what we should do, but so often we avoid the thing that could benefit us most. It's a mystery of mankind; in fact, did you know that humans are the only living creature that will willingly become less than they ought to become? Ask any person on their deathbed, particularly those who've lived a long life, what they wish they would have done with their life. Of the many different answers, there's five pieces of wisdom that we should all learn about:

1. I wish I wouldn't have compared myself to others.
2. I wish I would have taken action and dove head-first.
3. I wish I would have tuned the world out more.

4. I wish I didn't wait to "start it tomorrow."
5. I wish I would have taken more chances.

I think a gem of life wisdom is to begin with the end in mind. When you're out of shape, or even in shape, and you have a goal for where you want to be or where you want to go, begin with the end in mind. Imagine the fitness capacity to climb that mountain, run that race, or fit into those clothes that you haven't worn in ten years. Be inspired and visualize those moments. Better yet, when you die, because the mortality rate for all of us is 100%, have you decided where you are going to go?

As a parent, this is where things get even trickier. You see, most people struggle mightily with themselves with the aforementioned "own worst enemy" stuff, but then we have kids and raise them with our "own worst enemy" habits and then infect them with our own shortcomings on top of their own. Just try to imagine this for one second. You struggle mightily in an area of your life, let's say health and fitness, because this is a common one. You make poor eating choices and it shows, and you live a rather sedentary lifestyle. Then you have a kid or three who begins to play sports and it becomes apparent that they are behind their peers because they too are rather sedentary and don't eat well. How were they to know? The environment they grew up in modeled that for them. But here's where it gets messy, Mom and Dad begin to preach to them that they need to eat better and begin working out so they can get better at their sport. Can you imagine their confusion and why they may not be excited or may even resist this? Kids aren't dumb, they are quite smart and can sense a hypocrite a mile away. The defiance then angers the parent, not because of the defiance, but because it's a misinterpreted conviction of their own efforts. Think about it, when we are confronted with our own shortcomings in another person, we often judge them. The Bible even talks about this in the book of Matthew 7:3-5:

> Why do you look at the speck of sawdust in your brother's eye and pay no attention to the plank in your own eye? How can you say to your brother, let me take the speck out of your eye, when all the time there is a plank in your own eye? You hypocrite! First take the plank out of your own eye, and then you will see clearly to remove the speck from your brother's eye.

So why am I writing about all this "own worst enemy" and "begin with the end in mind" talk? It's because Livia reveals to me my own shortcomings and hypocritical tendencies. She reveals to me how flawed I am at times. The interesting irony about this is society, or "the world" as I like to refer to it, would likely characterize Livia as flawed, disabled, or mentally challenged. But if anyone should be labeled as such, it should be me. Though I am actively working to improve these flaws, I am the one who has a short temper and loses his cool. I'm the one who judges others. I'm the one who cares too much about what other people think of me. I am the one who compares himself to others. Livia does none of these things. While the world may categorize her as devolved, her and other special needs humans, when you really think of it, are quite a bit further evolved than most of us "regular folks." We are stricken with all sorts of worldly concerns and calamities, while my beautiful princess exists in this peaceful present state. Never judging, never cursing, always watching, ever listening, and just being. And when her emotions are triggered, she'll cry, no-holds-barred style. Wouldn't it be great to live like that? To never judge, curse, to observe, to listen, and to just be free of comparison, impatience, anxiety, and stress. Furthermore, when it's time to cry, we actually just let it flow and not be fearful of the judgement that comes from that emotion (I'm talking to you, tough guy). All I know is that I want to live more like Livia does. She's the closest thing to Jesus that I've ever met.

18 FOCUS

Have you ever watched somebody's eyes when staring out the window of a car that is driving fast, or a plane that is about to take off, or how about on the Gravitron? You know, you remember that carnival ride that spun so fast and everyone dared you to go on it and not puke? Yeah, that one. Remember other peoples' eyes darting right to left or left to right trying to capture objects as they were flying by? This is a bit like Livia's eyes when she's having a bout with Nystagmus. Nystagmus is a vision condition in which the eyes make repetitive, uncontrolled movements. These movements often result in reduced vision and depth perception and can affect balance and coordination. These involuntary eye movements can occur from side to side, up and down, or in a circular pattern. This kind of throws you for a loop if you've been around her for the first time and her eyes are darting all over the place. I've seen the look of wonder, confusion, and empathy on other people's faces when this is happening. We always appreciate it when loving family and friends ask questions about stuff like this rather than just trying to act like they don't notice it or feel like it would make it weird to ask. Curiosity shows that you are trying to understand and learn, which is really special to Livia, because she wants you to feel comfortable around her and talk to her and even hold her! She's very social, it's just different! But if you could just break through that initial, uncomfortable wall, I promise there is such beauty in a relationship with someone with special needs. It transcends the normal relationships and it just goes to another level. It's difficult to describe, but if you have a child or have befriended a special needs person, you know what I'm talking about.

So last night we were having family movie night. My son, Brooks, is very goal-oriented, so during quarantine due to COVID-19, my wife has been setting reading goals for him. For every five books he reads, he gets something or gets to do something. It may be a treat, it may be to go fishing, and for this particular incentive, he got to pick a family movie. Turns out he didn't get to pick, Daddo got to pick. I told Brooks, "Hey champ, how about *The Karate Kid* (the one with Jackie Chan and Jaden Smith)?"

Brooks wasn't into it, "Noooooooooooo!"
He wanted to watch a slough of cartoon movies, but not *The Karate Kid*. I don't give up that easily though, so I pressed forward. "Dude, we've been talking and training to be a warrior kid, don't you want to watch a movie about one?"
"Nooooooo!" He responded again.
I knew he needed to watch this film and I knew he'd love it, so I wasn't about to budge. Momma sweetened the pot for him with, "Hey buddy, how about Momma makes some popcorn and we'll watch It?"

"Yeah, that sounds good," he said with a smile on his face.

We didn't hear a peep from him as soon as we pressed play. He was locked in, and so was I! The LaRue men have a unique ability to tune out the world if a good action movie is on the TV. COVID-19 could turn into a zombie apocalypse with zombies busting through my window into my home, and I'd still be there mouth open, drooling, and glued to the story on the screen.

We had recently got a Henzinger collar for Livia to wear when she's sitting to give her neck support from bobbleheading all over the place. You'd probably recognize the concept, as it was originally invented for football players at the University of Michigan to wear on the top of their shoulder pads to limit stingers and concussions. I just randomly said to my wife, "Honey, let's put that neck pad thing on Livia and I'll sit with her so she can watch the movie also." I wasn't thinking that anything profound would occur, I just wanted to snuggle with the little lady. About 30 minutes into the movie I was drooling on top of her head and she was sitting in the gap of my "Indian Style" sitting position. I glanced down and also saw her fixated on the movie. No nystagmus, no head moving right to left, just dialed in on the movie. She was taking it all in and was so focused. I'd never seen her like this! I whispered to Momma sitting behind me, "She's watching Momma!" Tears welled up in my eyes and I just bowed my head and began praying and thanking God for this moment and pleading for breakthrough and more moments like this. As I lifted my head from my prayer, I commenced the open-mouth, drooling stare as the karate kid pulled off an incredible upset, and I never even saw it comin! ☐

So what's the lesson she taught me? The lesson was to stabilize and focus! The Lord almighty is the same yesterday, the same today, and the same tomorrow. That, my friends, is called stability. Once Livia's neck was stabilized and she didn't need to focus on her head wavering this way and that, she was able to focus her attention on the use of her eyes and use those brown beauties to watch a story of a young boy overcoming adversity. Once you have stability, you can now use that newfound strength to focus on the things that truly matter. When your life is mass chaos and you're trying to do everything yourself, there's no stability! There's another "S" word for that, and it's called STRESS! It's probably causing you to have focus nowhere and it's likely killing you slowly. Seek stability in the Lord, and then focus your eyes on the overcomer. Only then will you find true peace, focus, and joy.

19 LONELINESS

Are humans the only animals that cry? This is a question I was curious about and it turns out, I'm not the only one. This is a question that many people have wondered over time, and with good reason. "If you define crying as expressing grief or joy, then the answer is yes. Animals do create tears, but only to lubricate their eyes," says Bryan Amaral, senior curator of the Smithsonian's National Zoo. It's quite interesting when you begin to do a little studying on this topic. You can dive down a neuropsychology trail and evolutionary theory and plenty of arguments will arise that try to describe why humans are the only animals that cry from emotion. The problem with science, and I'm a fan of it (otherwise I wouldn't have spent a fortune on studying a branch of science for seven years), is there are no absolutes. Sure, there can be well-constructed arguments, called theories, that have proven things to be close to fact. But there's always this space, big or small, that leaves no absolutes when it comes to science. Albert Einstein even said:

> The scientific theorist is not to be envied. For Nature, or more precisely experiment, is an inexorable and not very friendly judge of his work. It never says 'Yes' to a theory. In the most favorable cases it says 'Maybe,' and in the great majority of cases simply 'No.' If an experiment agrees with a theory it means the latter 'Maybe,' and if it does not agree it means 'No.' Probably every theory will someday experience its 'No' – most theories [do], soon after conception."

Crying is something we can all relate to, and if you haven't cried in a very long time, I'm worried for you. Crying is actually well documented to be healthy for you. Crying detoxifies the body, self soothes by activating the parasympathetic nervous system (PNS), dulls pain by releasing oxytocin and other endorphins, improves mood, rallies support from others, helps recover from grief, and restores emotional balance. I cry a few times per week usually, and it's not because I'm a health and fitness nerd and I'm looking for the aforementioned benefits. It's not like I set time aside to have little cry sessions in between my sets of kettlebell swings, although crying in a training session has certainly happened before. I think I cry often because I aim to live inspired and with my heart on my sleeve. I really care a lot about other people, and when you invest, serve, and care for others, you've invested a lot of emotional energy into others. Is there any other way to live than this way? I know it hurts sometimes, but that's what makes us human and God's unique creation. When someone I know is hurting, it hurts me. When I watch something in a movie that is sad, or more oftentimes joyful, tears well up in my eyes. Or when I'm watching my children, singing to my daughters before bed, or praying with my son, I just get overwhelmed with emotion and the tears flow. I can just think of my beautiful bride right now and how rich she's made my life, and I can turn on the tears quickly. I'm not sure why I'm this way or why others are more stoic and able to hold the tears back, but this I do know without debate, crying is good for you.

With Livia, it's a bit different. She certainly cries, and man oh man, you should hear her roar when she really gets going. She has this high-pitch screech when she's really worked up that I swear could shatter glass. Like I've stated before, as a man, patience is something I struggle with. Interestingly though, my lack of patience doesn't lead to me quitting. This may sound like I'm stroking my own ego here, but I have this rare combination of lack of patience combined with mosquito-like persistence. I mean you gotta tip your cap to the 'ol mosquito. They are persistent. Where I'm going with that is I used to get incredibly frustrated with Livia when she'd cry because she couldn't communicate to me what was wrong, at least that's what my lack of patience was telling me. The truth is, Livia probably was growing frustrated with me and perhaps has a bit of her Dad in her. I can imagine her saying, "F'real Daddo? I mean I'm either hungry, have a full diaper, am uncomfortable, sick, or tired. Just go through that simple checklist, and you'll figure it out!" Most of the time that would work. However, there were times that it wouldn't, and I'd be left frantically trying to figure it out, 'cause you know, that's what us guys try to do. Then it dawned on me one day, there's another reason Livia cries, and it's out of loneliness. It doesn't happen very often, but there are times when I know she feels lonely, even if she's just a few

101

feet away in the next room. The distance from another person isn't the only reason people feel lonely. Livia is loved immensely, but admittedly, sometimes she's just in the next room chilling and the rest of the family is in the kitchen. We are in eyesight of her, but she feels like she's not included. I'm sure you can relate to this, because once I shared Livia's perspective, it brought up memories of when I've felt this way. It breaks my heart that I had to learn this lesson from Livia all over again, but I'm grateful that I did.

The shortest verse in the Bible comes from John 11:35, and it simply says, "Jesus wept." These two simple words carry far more depth than any of us will likely comprehend, but it shows to me that the creator of the universe understands the human condition far better than we do. He created us after all, and He created us to be inclusive of one another, to love one another, and to cry with one another. I know someone who reads this will relate to Livia's lesson here in feeling alone; however, when you have a relationship with the King of Kings and Lord of Lords, you'll never be all alone. It's the most comforting thing that I've ever experienced, the unconditional love of our Father is available to everyone.

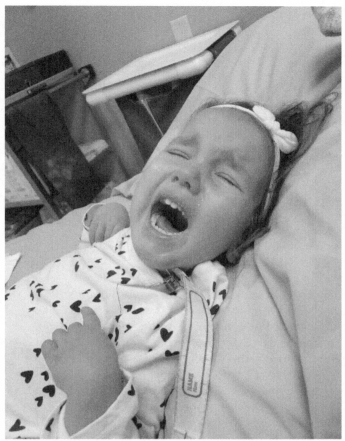

12: Livia sharing with the nurses her eardrum shattering warrior princess cry!

20 LOVE

You know how they say love is a verb and not an adjective? Or to put it another way, love is an action, not just a word. For example, I love my wife and kids something fierce, and even if I never said, "I love you" with my words, they should feel how much I love them (I hope) due to my actions and how I care for and even discipline (the kids, anyway) them. Now, there's something certainly special when someone tells you that they love you with their words. I'd hate to never hear the words "I love you, Daddo" from my wife or kids; however, there's one thing that I'd hate worse, and that's not feeling like they loved me.

You see, it's one thing to say "I love you," but it's quite another to show it. It's no different than when I coach people in business, fitness, or faith to walk the walk and not just talk the talk. The best case scenario though is when you can combine the two, talking the talk and walking the walk. When the two are combined, they are maximized and the spread of love continues. As Christians, we are called to evangelize, or share the good news about the gospel, which is basically God's truth about how much he dearly loves us, His creation. Jesus perfected the teaching or "the talk" part of love throughout his ministry, but nobody in the history of mankind has ever walked it out more perfectly and beautifully than Jesus did. It's why His truth and ministry are every bit as relevant, if not more so, today as it was over 2000 years ago.

Here's an interesting thing about Jesus though. In the Bible, it isn't recorded that Jesus actually says, "I love you," to anyone in particular. Crazy right!? God/Jesus is love, yet He never told anyone that he loved them? Now, it does say in the Bible in John 21:25, "...and there are also many other things that Jesus did, which if they were written one by one, I suppose that even the world itself could not contain the books that would be written. Amen." So it's very plausible that Jesus said "I love you" to his mother Mary and father Joseph, as well as His disciples; however, there is a chance that He did not, but He was an expert at showing it. Personally, I know without a shadow of doubt that Jesus Christ loves me fiercely; however, I've never heard his audible voice saying, "I love you, Brandon."

I dove down that trail of love with Jesus first, because no matter who reads this, no matter if they've never heard anyone tell them "I love you," they will know that Jesus loves them unconditionally. And secondly, because of Livia. She's closing in on the big girl age of five, and while we pray daily for her to develop the ability to walk, talk, and play, it hasn't been so yet. So, I've never actually heard my little warrior princess utter the words "I love you, Daddo." But Livia, like Jesus, has taught me how to receive love and give love without the use of words. She expresses it by being present with me, listening to me, smiling with me, crying with me, and laughing with me. Imagine if we did that with the people around us? It would change the world!

Fortunately for me, I do get to hear those four lovely words from my son, daughter, and my bride daily, but I'd give just about anything to hear those four beautiful words come out of Livia's mouth. But here's the interesting thing, there's something especially strong about the speechless love given from her. It's a brand of love that's so unique, genuine, and pure, and the only thing I can liken it to, is the love that I also feel from Jesus…speechless, unique, genuine, and pure.

13: Livia showing me that LOVE is an action, and not just an adjective. We can LOVE each other daily by our actions, and that is a much stronger brand of love than just saying the words "I Love you."

ABOUT THE AUTHOR

Brandon is a follower of Christ, a devoted husband, a passionate father, a loyal friend, a transformational coach, a health and performance expert, a competitive life athlete, a plate spinning entrepreneur, transparent speaker, a zealous outdoorsman, a social media positivity activist, and a greenhorn author.

He attended undergraduate school at Minnesota State University – Mankato as an underachieving student athlete while studying Exercise Science. He later attended graduate school at A.T. Still University, where he received his Master's in Human Movement/Strength and Conditioning. His experiences and personal development have led to eclectic work and business experiences. He's coached athletes ranging from youth to professional, and he has coached even more "regular," also known as "life athletes," people ranging from sedentary to the fitness freak. He also runs a human performance brand called Well Built Humans, where he offers corporate wellness coaching, speaking engagements, fitness bootcamp, online kettlebell coaching, team character building, nutrition/supplement coaching, and kettlebells.

Brandon recently moved back to his hometown of La Crescent, Minnesota, to be closer to his family and get involved in what he refers to as a "sleeping giant" of a community. In his spare time, he loves to bowhunt just about anything and fish for everything.

Brandon is known for his genuine and transparent personality, and if you spend any amount of time with him, he will likely challenge you to get better.

Made in the USA
Monee, IL
27 June 2020

34897371R00069